CODING IS EVERYWHERE

Coding in Video Games

by Elizabeth Noll

BLASTOFF! 2 READERS

BELLWETHER MEDIA • MINNEAPOLIS, MN

Note to Librarians, Teachers, and Parents:

Blastoff! Readers are carefully developed by literacy experts and combine standards-based content with developmentally appropriate text.

Level 1 provides the most support through repetition of high-frequency words, light text, predictable sentence patterns, and strong visual support.

Level 2 offers early readers a bit more challenge through varied simple sentences, increased text load, and less repetition of high-frequency words.

Level 3 advances early-fluent readers toward fluency through increased text and concept load, less reliance on visuals, longer sentences, and more literary language.

Level 4 builds reading stamina by providing more text per page, increased use of punctuation, greater variation in sentence patterns, and increasingly challenging vocabulary.

Level 5 encourages children to move from "learning to read" to "reading to learn" by providing even more text, varied writing styles, and less familiar topics.

Whichever book is right for your reader, Blastoff! Readers are the perfect books to build confidence and encourage a love of reading that will last a lifetime!

This edition first published in 2019 by Bellwether Media, Inc.

No part of this publication may be reproduced in whole or in part without written permission of the publisher. For information regarding permission, write to Bellwether Media, Inc., Attention: Permissions Department, 6012 Blue Circle Drive, Minnetonka, MN 55343.

Library of Congress Cataloging-in-Publication Data

Names: Noll, Elizabeth, author.
Title: Coding in Video Games / by Elizabeth Noll.
Description: Minneapolis, MN : Bellwether Media, Inc., 2019. | Series:
   Blastoff! Readers. Coding Is Everywhere | Includes bibliographical
   references and index. | Audience: Ages 5 to 8. | Audience: Grades K to 3.
Identifiers: LCCN 2017060191 (print) | LCCN 2017060780 (ebook) | ISBN
   9781626178366 (hardcover : alk. paper) | ISBN 9781618914804
   (pbk. : alk. paper) | ISBN 9781681035772 (ebook)
Subjects: LCSH: Video games–Programming–Juvenile literature.
Classification: LCC QA76.76.C672 (ebook) | LCC QA76.76.C672 N65 2019 (print)
   | DDC 794.8/1525–dc23
LC record available at https://lccn.loc.gov/2017060191

Editor: Christina Leaf   Designer: Brittany McIntosh

Printed in the United States of America, North Mankato, MN

Table of Contents

Coding in Video Games

Super Mario Odyssey

Have you ever wanted to make a video game?

First, write your ideas down. Then you must learn how to write **code**.

All video games use code. It tells the computer what to do. This makes the game work.

▶BUY
SELL
QUIT

Welcome! How help you?

Pokémon Crystal

```
AzaleaMart_MapScripts:
    .SceneScripts:
8           db 0
9
                                    Pokémon Crystal
                                      source code
10  .MapCallbacks:
11          db 0
12

13  AzaleaMartClerkScript:
            opentext
            pokemart MARTTYPE_STA
            closetext
            end


      CooltrainerMScript:
             faceplayer Az
```

Humans write code in
programming languages.

Sonic Mania

Code controls everything
in a video game. It creates
the look of backgrounds,
characters, and items.

It helps players catch balls or sell cakes!

NBA 2K18

The History of Coding in Video Games

Tennis for Two

The first video game was *Tennis for Two*. A scientist invented it in 1958 to make his science fair exciting.

The **program** was very simple.

Tennis for Two
at the science fair

In 1962, researchers created the first computer game. Then, **BASIC** was invented in 1964. This language made creating computer games easy.

Spacewar!, the first computer game

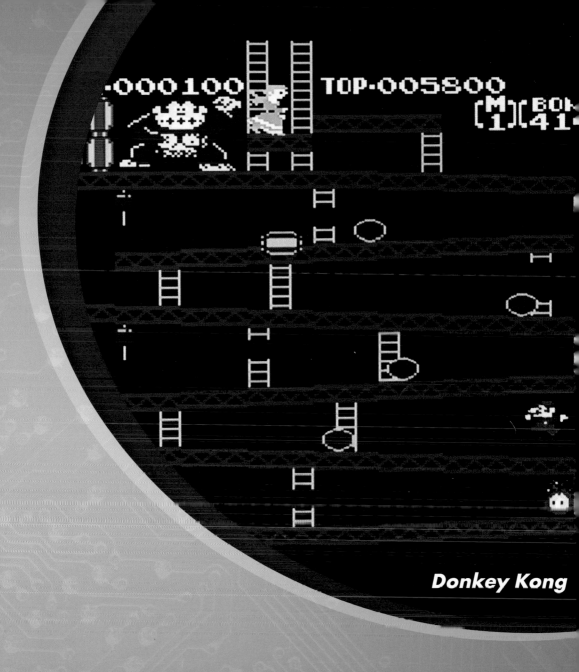

Donkey Kong

Later languages made games like *Frogger* and *Donkey Kong* possible.

The Legend of Zelda:
Breath of the Wild

Today's video games are
fancier than the early games.

Game designers write code in languages like **Java** and **C++**.

Minecraft

How Does Coding Work in Video Games?

Mario Kart 8 Deluxe

How does code work in the popular game *Mario Kart 8*? It does everything!

You can change
a kart's speed,
direction, or color
because of code.

Code also controls how characters move. This is **animation**. Code tells the computer how far and which way to move the characters.

Play Mario Kart 8

hold A:
code tells kart to go

hold B:
kart goes backwards

move joystick right:
code moves the kart
right to get the item

move joystick left:
miss the item!

press L:
code says to use
the item

press R:
kart jumps

Can you picture the video game you want to invent?

Scratch game

Scratch code

```
when     clicked
set  CatScore ▼ to 0
set size to 50 %
forever
    go to mouse-pointer ▼
    if      touching Robot1 ▼ ?   t
        play sound meow ▼ until
        if      CatScore > 
```

Code can bring your game
to life!

Glossary

animation—code that controls how objects move in a game

BASIC—a programming language that is easy to use; BASIC stands for Beginner's All-purpose Symbolic Instruction Code.

C++—a difficult programming language that allows a lot of control

code—instructions for a computer

Java—a programming language that works on many different machines

program—a set of rules for a computer that performs a specific function

programming languages—special languages that humans use to talk to computers

To Learn More

AT THE LIBRARY
Kelly, James Floyd. *The Story of Coding*. New York, N.Y.: DK Publishing, 2017.

Lyons, Heather. *Programming Games and Animation*. Minneapolis, Minn.: Lerner Publications, 2017.

Wainewright, Max. *Code Your Own Games!: 20 Games to Create with Scratch*. New York, N.Y.: Sterling Children's Books, 2017.

ON THE WEB
Learning more about coding in video games is as easy as 1, 2, 3.

1. Go to www.factsurfer.com.

2. Enter "coding in video games" into the search box.

3. Click the "Surf" button and you will see a list of related web sites.

With factsurfer.com, finding more information is just a click away.

Index

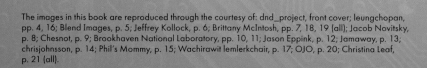

The images in this book are reproduced through the courtesy of: dnd_project, front cover; leungchopan, pp. 4, 16; Blend Images, p. 5; Jeffrey Kollock, p. 6; Brittany McIntosh, pp. 7, 18, 19 (all); Jacob Novitsky, p. 8; Chesnot, p. 9; Brookhaven National Laboratory, pp. 10, 11; Jason Eppink, p. 12; Jamaway, p. 13; chrisjohnsson, p. 14; Phil's Mommy, p. 15; Wachirawit lemlerkchair, p. 17; OJO, p. 20; Christina Leaf, p. 21 (all).